I am mesmerized by this book. I have rarely ~~~~~~ ~~~~~ ~~ ~~~~
in a poet's language as I am reading T.J. Anderson's unrelenting symphony
of American diction, American history, and the visceral realities of his
American experience. These poems buzz with wordplay, dance with lingo,
shimmy with imagery. Just as much as all that, they are unflinching in their
wisdom about race, about class, about all the violence and discord in our
American culture.
—Jaswinder Bolina, author of *Of Color* and *The 44th of July*

T.J. Anderson III turns shards of memory into poems we can never
forget—fleshy, raw, intimate poems that cut to the bone and cradle the
heart. He summons worlds of violence and violins, revealing the secrets of
a culture capable of surviving the multiple pandemics that made his world
and our own. To the readers who did not know Anderson was one of
America's greatest contemporary poets ... *t/here it is.*
—Robin D. G. Kelley, author of *Thelonious Monk: The Life and Times of
an American Original*

"Must the devil have all the good tunes," asks composer John Adams.
T.J. Anderson III, who knows and can teach us a thing or two about the
music, hears poet/pianist Cecil Taylor coming from a place "where the
devil gives up his hold of the music." The devil's loss, that devil we know,
is all to our gain. t/here it is turns out to be a place somewhere "between
spoken and vernacular," a place where phonemes congregate, arranging
themselves into new melodies/meanings, even pronunciations. These are
poems that tune your ears, and turn them towards the new good news.
—A.L. Nielsen, poet, critic, and editor of Lorenzo Thomas's award-
winning posthumous work, *Don't Deny My Name: Words, Music and the
Black Intellectual Tradition*

t/here it is

Cover art by Joseph Epps

Cover typeface: Futura
Interior typeface: Garamond Premier Pro

Cover design by Laura Joakimson and
Interior design by Ken Keegan

Library of Congress Cataloging-in-Publication Data

Names: Anderson, T. J., III, 1958- author.
Title: T/here it is / T.J. Anderson III.
Other titles: There it is
Description: Oakland, California : Omnidawn Publishing, 2022. | Summary:
    "In t/here it is, poet T. J. Anderson III describes the struggle to
    articulate an autobiographical journey of mind and heart through the
    vehicle of poetry. With a voice that is fueled by an African American
    aesthetic, Anderson negotiates his continual coming of age in a place
    that is often bent on destroying his identity. These poems resist and
    subsequently celebrate their right to exist on their own terms. Each
    poem challenges the need to create a linguistically informed tonality
    that speaks to the shifting experiences and perceptions of history:
    personal, cultural, national, and spiritual. The poetry in this
    collection takes shape in multiple ways as each section contributes to
    various installations of memory"-- Provided by publisher.

Identifiers: LCCN 2022035001 | ISBN 9781632431073 (trade paperback)
Subjects: BISAC: POETRY / General | POETRY / American / African American &
    Black | LCGFT: Poetry.
Classification: LCC PS3551.N39477 T44 2022 | DDC 811/.54--dc23/eng/20220721
LC record available at https://lccn.loc.gov/2022035001

Published by Omnidawn Publishing, Oakland, California
www.omnidawn.com   (510) 237-5472
10 9 8 7 6 5 4 3 2 1
ISBN: 978-1-63243-107-3

t/here it is

T. J. Anderson III

OMNIDAWN PUBLISHING
OAKLAND, CALIFORNIA
2022

Previously Published Books

Devonte Travels the Sorry Route, Omnidawn Publishing, 2019.

Cairo Workbook, Established Author Series, Willow Books, 2014.

River to Cross, The Backwaters Press, 2009.

Notes to Make the Sound Come Right: Four Innovators of Jazz Poetry, University of Arkansas Press, 2004.

At Last Round Up, Chapbook Series, lift books, 1996.

Atibon Legba louvri bayé pou mwen

For the Ancestors.

Deep gratitude to my parents.

All art is collaborative.

Table of Contents

From an embankment, a rise and a palpitation, two leggeds astride four leggeds.

—Ahrayamé

That silent beat makes the drumbeat, it makes the drum, it makes the beat. Without it there is no drum, no beat.... you hear it in between, its sound is.

—Bob Kaufman

A whisper is a shout, modified to suit the darkness.

—Édouard Glissant

Notes is good enough for you people, but us likes a mixtery.

—an ex-slave from the Georgia Sea Islands

Poetics

A poem is a geode:
She was at the faucet,
filling a glass of water.

I am concerned about the vast immeasurable space between wor(l)ds:
He was at the table,
his face lost to print.

The unseen permeation of things within things:
There was a tabby at her feet,
tail erect and purring.

Systems within systems:
An ant made its way
across the table.

All manner of being and nonbeing:
There was a hint of smoke
coming out of the toaster.

All implications and motivations:
They both looked up
at each other.

All mechanizations that cannot be classifiable:
She turned off the faucet.
He put down the paper.

Under a rubric of terms:
There was a knock at the door.
The phone began to ring.

I
/ˈflôrˌbôrd/

What's in a Name?

In his memoir Up from the Cane Breaks, *David Dewitt Turpeau, my great grandfather writes of my Martiniqan ancestors dropping the "x" in the family name and changing it from Turpeaux to Turpeau.*

X—Denoting any unknown or unspecified variable factor, number, person, or thing.
                                        —Collins English Dictionary

If a flag catch fire and an X burn in. That "X" believe me is black.
                                        —Amiri Baraka

Cut cane cut skin cut time
Cut circuitous route cut colt cut
Gilded man skin cut me to the quick
I'm an albatross skirting stormy seas
Coloratura cut in the volcanic heave
of triangle trade Caribbean cut

So tell me, what's in a name? The old
Shakespearean twist of fate, the tender fold of mandible
enunciating the inheritance of a weighty consonant?
Perhaps the Sisyphusian push, reckoner of lost continents
home wrecker to colonial pulse.
From bicep curve to bipedal cargo
from haul to hull each shinning
ship from see to sea
from an alchemy of chains
a Calibanic braille? A limbo in the entrails of a slaver?

Limbo. N.4 a West Indian dance in which dancers pass while leaning backwards, under a bar.
Origin uncertain but is said to have originated after the experience of the cramped condition between the slave-ship decks of the Middle Passage.

19

What then is the identifier, the irons?
The premier vowel, the family legacy,
The jewel so to speak hinged in the throat?
Preamble utterance, a logos divine brimming,
the Anthurium's pollenated discharge?
Label of owner or ancestor, the notion
I mean nation to live up to.
What then they call you by, the adjectives
that follow your back to the slack wood of a Louisiana auction block.
The well-placed desk, carved out well of ink.
The ledger.

―――

In the classroom, the teacher's roll call,
smudged report card summary to
what you've now retained. Job stub paycheck
nine to five brutal brunt.
Tell me, how does one step into that?
How does one own up to a name?
X I'm my father's son
My sun's flower
My fallow dung
X My mother's boy
My monsoon's boil
My muttered buoy
X My sister's brother
My cistern's brothel
X My cousins' cousin
My cow pen cussing

Cut
Comrade to the teaming legions
of cells writhing beneath my feet.
Unarticulated, this Impulse to take back.
To lift the ink
off the manifest
New World bound.

There are Rivers
The sky is a river

global daffodils hold where

sky strikes and swells

bounty blue
(it's a reign of wind and water
and mama held my hand, led me out)

seaweed in her hair seaweed in her cloud, her storm, her laugher

she introduced me to spontaneous tumble
of legs and laughter

and there I held on when the current

pulled me under

On a grassy slope alight with
patter and pigment
butterflies tangle in lavender

song birds (if you imagine them)
dandelion stream snake your way
through the locks of memory
rock steady the course of ancient stones

we will still be here

open hearted, recognizable
by the gifts we give each other
we will be in the place where
our arms cradle up cornucopia of stars

she invokes Nut her body night
sky sings us into creation.

(in the darkness I hear the waves whisper)

feet sink into ancestral clay
breathe and an ocean's forest bears witness
singing the compost of Babylon

there are rivers (if you imagine them)

dusky and ancient
sold to soul to broth to bone
a life where roots
uncover their bloody blooms.
And yet...

The Channel

My house squats on stilts
& skirts sorrowful seas.

> *Is it a crane, for I can see its white wings?*

No. It is a barkentine brimmed with bodies.
The white you see are sails.

> *But, I also see white specks*
> *prickling through the floor.*

Holding up a spyglass, he whispered "Re-jec-ta-men-ta."

~~~

The jaw of land juts out
Lost crust of memory fuels my eyes

I hear an animal hoarseness
where an Orisha's voice comes careening through

My body in deep fever, temperate zone
My belly a peninsula
snared by each knowing spasm

Limbs that reach for a mere atom of space
The sea's muzzle rabid with foam
devourer of time chewing barnacle pocked wood

The chronicles are empty, save for what
I retain in my memory
Mediated through music
a sonic fabric unwound
in search of the loop
to fit my needle through

Kapalango drum's taut skin

Rhythms that pick up my pulmonary cadence
Tongue that weaves across a balafon of teeth
Ahh, the stimulant of your future face

Does the air taste of salt?

No it's metallic and heavy
Sweat bile, blood bone
Scabs that pulsate and fester
Pestilence putrid

Unnamable urges
to tongue me out

Who witnesses this?

Faces on the deck
Phantoms white dis-ghosts
Retrievers of property
I slip the railings

Stares to envy my drowning
Foam and wave curl
Dark rhythm that laps the hold's edges
Fish/brine/albatross/ and bow head/ spray.

Are we moving forward?

Dipped arm folded to prayer
Lungs engorged I see them
before I go asunder
I was an arm waving
a limb cutting through the air
stirring foam in my wake

The Porch Sweepers

This world here is a blesséd and dangerous place.
—Arahyamé

Who are those people who

                step out each morning

with broom to front porch

sweeping
away the last
remnants of night

Gazing at
        either dark clouds
                or sun

shoeless or slippered

where the
foot pulses
    weight
      on grieving floorboards
who hold in their grain the witness/the witless/the whiteness
to what is human

                          Those former trees/
                          those formal lives/

those floating leaves:
//splintered//spractured//serrated//
from large forests
where sharp beaked birds
perched & preened.

The portrait is not pretty
The portrait is not petty
and this thing/this text/this tome/this taunter
/this textile/this tactile/this tactful
/this tenderloin/this turnkey/this turnip/
This poem stalled and started
off in celebration
of the lone sweeper
diligently dismantling cobwebs

Hoping for an ever /a never/ an evergreen /an epistle
/an epoxy /an ember/
a tomorrow of sunset laced postcards
& glowing sons who've stolen keys
& driven off in bronco busting cars
towards fortresses of gutted mountains
mainlines/mainstays/municipalities/
mockumentaries/motherfuckers/
managerial/myopic/melatonin/

& dear, dear Aunt Myrtle who waited
all this time at the beach
for her tide to come in

                                            and
                            when it did

she realized that we
all are a species
of ravagers gouging
our way through
crystalline geodes who
hold in their mouths
the secrets of Earth's
golden embassy.

Oble Tanbou I

A pileated woodpecker pecks
                        out sixteenth notes on a dead poplar.

                Reminds me was that one
                                invented first flute.
                                        Rhythm as
resistance syncopated

                                        drum way- out thru
primordial octave.

This here be wood song
This here be chopper's chant

Oble Tanbou
Oble Tanbou

Soon the ancient ones will arrive
to take us through their paces
serenade the earth with
their tongue-toked language.

As an initiate, I've been raised
to measure
this balm of séance
Oble Tanbou
To linger in its magic
lift flute to mouth
Oble Tanbou
Let wood cradle lips
to let loose a fragile blow
to evoke a plaintive lament under
a canopy of impenetrable clouds.

Oble Tanbou
Oble Tanbou
Oble Tanbou

                              In this historical horizon
                    I conjure shacks and shanties
          writhing up
                         from salt splintered decks

My memory, a talisman that slips
between corpses

                                        No ocean in the wood
          Oble Tanbou

          but a sea of timber and topsoil

slipping away into the mouth
of a whirlpool

Oble Tanbou

                                        It's slipping away

to where
my anguished lament
loses its potency

Unable to wrestle the gulf of epochs
my saga is simply a matter
of believing beyond retrieving

See I'm trying to initiate
a poem here
but I need space.

Oble Tanbou
Oble Tanbou

                    I need room
                    to exercise
                    my pioneer spit

and spirit.
Oble Tanbou
Oble Tanbou

Find a place where
my witnessed absence
spews from my mouth
like an avalanche of lungs
in a coal mine,
like a peck of Taoists
sun tied to a steel rail
like a stampede of Black
bodies ignited by fire
and commemorative postcards

II

A ridge of sea washed bones cast red shadows.
Jagged rib cages
look like raw cathedral spires
and a tree lined shore turns magically
into ledgers where my mother tongue vanishes

                                        My feet tell me
that this was once the place
where rivers swept through, but where did they go?
Too many bodies of water to recall?

They lead to chains
                    with each eddy

                                        turbulent/unforgiving

Now the news comes in telling us it's a virus
Seeding destruction in its wake
and I don't know which one

they're referring to, Cause, see I never
cottoned too much to being called an American
when cross waters smoke fires
bodies pillaged by disease.

III

                              While these woods may betray a calm
there is an anger deep inside me

                              Ancient as anything I care to know

& I'm grasping for breath
& I'm grasping for words
& I'm grasping for sense
& I'm grasping for that place of solace

where just that one pileated bird
routinely taps for grubs on a dead limb
scalloped and pock marked.

It could be an oar to dip in the ocean.
It could be a wail beneath the decks
It could be the whisper of wind through bone
or the blood blue glare of a police cruiser
on a rain soaked night.

It could be an abacus
to record my vanishing.

II
/'spidl/

Newsprint

Words become parched
syllabic snippets to be parceled out
—hung over a stutterer's tongue
meant to branch off somewhere
between spoken and vernacular
—the wheel that morphs its way
the façade of gentle negotiations
where we mutter through
—and yes I've been misunderstood
on many occasions by those who profess
to have a filigree of hipness
—when the shake turns to sleight of hand
—the pen levels the parchment or the boat
backs up to Plymouth rock
this knowledge that they
bubble up with the words
and worlds of alterations
altercations of fecal documents
stained by triggers pulled so many years ago
—they even named a fancy horse after it
—rode out into the sunset city slicker style
—settled for suburban borders to insure
the only thing black was what emanated
from their stereos or what they smothered
behind the disco light of a cop's cruiser.

The Last Romantic

She sauntered against pale moon
Unveiled the universe to be a field
of blue butterflies harvest sprung

He sprouted from back city streets
Hystorical to the point
that anxiety dictated his origins

There was a broken bench
in Bearden Park where wood
edged up to look like a warm palm

The two of them sat
and thought about holding hands
But the prospect of

what to say on a night like this
where clichés rose as bright
as petals among shooting stars

Visions that brought them
to fireplace and homesteads
the river merchant wife's unlocked gate

A stream of grey naiads spun
ghosted a gauze around the beaker
of his trembling lips.

Words about to arise.

Drive/Bye

Big Eddie had the fright of his life
when a bullet flew
into his kitchen window
almost made Darlene a widow
when the missive went through
he was peering inside

his refrigerator less than five feet away
or was it five minutes
or five o'clock shadow
of a non-shaver (it was a Sunday)
or was it Jimmy Rushing singing
Russian Lullaby with Basie's back up

or was it Florida where he once
dreamed of snorkeling in red coral
but a bullet came flying through
just above the sink
and went through
those layers of glass and screen
or was it Big Eddie reaching for a glass

(I think he was about to pour
some milk) or was it the smudges on his
bifocals from the day he cried when
Darlene said she had planned long ago on leaving
but there was no evidence of departure
other than an entire window sending
tiny shards to the linoleum floor.

"When a bullet comes
through the window,
it ain't got no name
on it. Scared
the hell out of me."

postlude
The shots that shook
Big Eddie killed another
man in the street
in front of the building.

Bar Fly

Within the onslaught of sixteenth notes
we utter no first names here
nor knot the sound of our
dorsal knowing an ancient font
darkly poised on the page,
a header line drive that shimmies
slides language raw across the plate
or shuffles along to Blake's tin pan
alley tap piano roll, a finger F
sharped, shrapneled palpus.

At our local sports bar an armada
of screens floats up our desire for red automobiles
designer women that would deafen Odysseus.
While in the crib I fancied the constellations of Miro:
My parents constructed paper Cassiopeias
appended to black thread
while the hi-fi waxed Basie
and Mr. Five by Five
came barreling in.

To say I know nothing of this sporting life
proffered where speculators debate
averages and discourse on home ruin hits
is to deny the season ticket holder's garden tail spin.

So tell me kind bartender
about late night bruises
the sink rim with broke teeth
and aurora borealis blood spittle
or was that a nightingale?

I mistook you for saying *for the delight of the game*
and all the while I thought you were talking
brightly plumed pheasants,
gleaming plates of wild boar,
red potatoes from soil freshly sprung.

No Yoke

@ Beat Museum, San Francisco

I'm no beast of burden
no sidecar hustler
knocking on the rail
of Telegraph's incline
No slippery shyster
thieving to take your money
but I can surely tell
you the matter and the reason
why our shattered species struggles
is all contained in the back
lot of our boulder heads.
It's behind the glaciers in our eyes
and it looms and postulates
like some muddy obscene hipster
and spits out verdicts and condemnations
contradictions. Runs off and buys
postcards, poems, and shirts
plays the stocks and collects
all sorts of Beat memorabilia
thus making a glorious day
fraught with all matter
of impending disaster.

Fast Talking Hombre

After Anne Waldman's "Fast Talking Woman"

I'm a mountain range singer
I'm a maintain rage singer
I'm a mandible rift stinger

I'm the spinal rupture
that snakes up your back
I slam you into the ground.
You are in awe of my power.

I'm a moonlit serenader
I'm a macaw from Manassas
I'm a meadow from Muscogee

She was right. What's the point of lessoning, listing, listening?

Whatever it was made its way through
the corridor of states (staves?)

All bets were off,

"Gentlemen place your stakes on the floor!"

> *I'm out the door*
> *Oh, oh darling*
> *Oh, the state I'm in*
> *Oh, the state I'm in*

What's at stake is how we're going to preserve our democracy
(Devonte was laughing. Whoever saw it as such?)

*

I am the tongue dancer on the roof
of the world, quiver in the
cave of my mouth where I erupt

39

my volcanic spit
from sea to shining sea

My love is melodic necklace
that sets the intellect ablaze

I'm caller of urban cadences
Generator of fireside stories from the quarters
Hurler of vever verse to dance awake
the loa who never sleep

My song singes the scales
and ignites the propellants.
Don't act like this is the first time
you've heard of me!

III
/in'trans, en'trans/

Biblio/Biographie

I

Sidewalks deep lined
Caverns for fire
        ants

                        Step over a crack break your momma's
Red brick
     curve   the afternoon setting crimson

Any old house any odd house any outhouse any auld house
                                   on any college campus

                Call this one Langston University, established in 1897

This place to let set in an entire horizon afire
Oklahoma bovines Black Locust penned
              Constellations of gnats tail flicked,
                         murky watering troth
the gray opaque wing of a Damsel fly drowning

                   Momentary angelic this spit-spliff-split of land
this
    long-winded prairie view.

Breathe in the surfacesfacesherfaceherfacesurfaces & wirerywatery
waves of air
that writhes
        like an earthworm caught
Boomeranging in high heat.
        Point the way to the fffffffffffront door   home

long step upward for
this
      hesitant child caught in exotic rift

White door's gauze of brown dustings
high glass window a pair of eyes looking outward

unidentified by entrant this haunting
they peer through
regard his coming and going

II

Langston, Oklahoma, circa 1961

                                     i was three years old then

stepping off the back porch
steps that snake to a hard dirt trail.
Prairie grass and seed pod dance
leathery skinks brandishing their tails
shifting portraits sketched in Oklahoma dust.
It's a point of entry
an entrance entranced.
Hear I'm standing dumb

                                      but trying to speak.

III

Nashville, Tennessee, circa 1967

      When the door opens the floor shines
      to reveal novice fifty's suburban sways

      Commercials with something to slide
      on in stocking feet surfaces polished to politeness

shiny brown, almost rain slick
Balding ceiling above
Solitary (*solidarity forever. solidarity forever solidarity forever, for the union makes us strong*) instafamily

                                  (yellow bulb bracketing
parameters of shadows
holding it straight in seams of light and line.

A sliver of a figure against the wall,
perhaps a crystal's prism reset

Perhaps the contours of a face that lingers there
one's ancestor behind the mirror

The Frigidaire's plaintive moan in the next room

Willow weep for me weep in sympathy, etc. etc.

Blue gas glow of an Amana's speckled burners
kitchen table leg's cold arch of silver
the linoleum floor scalloped from walking

Perhaps a meal to engage an appetite
gastro gluttony *The Honeymooners* are on.
Gather 'round watch Ralph's threats to his wife (I forgot her name   )

Bistro and bestial buttered Colonial Bakery bread brown rimmed
Bakery that threatened the neighborhood
with delivery trucks of batter.
The plastic red transistor drowsy with AM news
incomprehensible these numbers
alchemic formulae mechanized in a nation of calculations

Tumultuous 1960's urban intersection
between traffic light and court stenographer.
Unclear window where the dial looms
just digits, quadrants pre agreed to by the
holders of the keys
the golden ones who recline in
their toxic light.
Who holds the hearth together?   ABC, CBS,
                                                    PBS
The way in is the way out the way out is the way in the way in is the way out
the way out is the

Please,

        can nothing be formed
        and made to stiffen
        this holy bodied boy?

Pretty Boy!

I was the anointed one
held up by a line
of lunch ladies who raised
their industrial spatulas and soup spoons
announcing the arrival of Pretty Boy!
And I sauntered in my tater tot
kingdom, resplendent
khakis and school books.
Prince of milk cartons
and tomato crowned meat loaf.
Sovereign of the stainless railings
we ran our trays through.

I fancied myself the envy
of pigtailed girls and
dungaree wearing boys.
Bouffanted and polyester teachers
craned for a glimpse of me
in their jeweled eye frames,
Witness to the presence of
such genius that would call
them to genuflect and all to go blind.
Yes, I was Pretty Boy
The elementary destroyer
The golden child
Ignorant to the years that would
eventually come to
wither away my magisterial beauty.

The Tennis Shoe Man Lives in Nashville

Last great stitch of celluloid
from the family Brownie
buck teeth & hard back books.
I was all Mr. Wizard's prepared slides
& chemistry sets, pearl colored
tusks of Pakistani elephants,
a Child's Garden of Verses,
Vivaldi's Four Seasons' continuous rattle
on the family High-Fi.
Cowboy pajamas, rodeo blanket with lasso prints
a six-gun made of clothespins
under my pillow to protect me.

Pigtailed Sharon Williams, whom I adored
told me once that he lived
across the street from our
parochial school playground
that I as a non-Catholic was particularly
susceptible to his dark sneers and rough hands
that neither Jaw Breakers, Bazooka Gum, nor Raisinets
taken in holy succession would remedy me
from his shoe strings tightening
around my throat.

She pointed to the yellow house on the corner
told me that was where he watched and waited.
Peering through weathered glass, sun faded curtains
I could see him there reclining
on a plastic covered couch
cheerfully whistling a tune
recently picked up from TV
a ploy to lure me in my schoolboy sweater
khaki shorted and spectacle wearing,
a young boy who still believed
in the sanctity of grown-ups.

The Wizard of Oz, 1965
for Janet

Two of us in the back
seat of a green station
wagon catapulting through Oklahoma.

A field of sun-cut poppies
bright as the wizard's balding pate.

>Then it was the balloon flung
>suddenly aloft, coat and tails,
>snake rope in the fray.

>*I don't know how it works.*
>*Bye-bye folks and I got them hogs to get in.*
>*The sooner you leave Oz*
>*the better you'll sleep, my dear.*

Daddy smokes fat Muriels to keep him
awake on the road, wheel traces tail lights of big rigs.

>*Only one thing I want you to do.*
>*What's that? Talk me out of it.*

So out of the window I follow
the Cimarron's maroon river flow.
Threaten to throw—up sunset blue horizon
Guthrie truck-stop gas thirty-one cents a gallon.
Guthrie truck-stop gas thirty-one cents a gallon.

>*'Twas Elmira Gulch first took my fancy*
>*not the floating jerseys in the pitch*
>*nor Zeke closing twister cellar hatch.*

My sister's hand swan dives into a bag of Fritos.
A big oil crane dips the prairie's blackness.
Sinclair   complimentary   dinnerware,
Sinclair   complimentary   dinnerware,

S&H Green stamps book my DNA,
wheat penny with the savior's face.

She bit her dog eh?

Ok, I'm guilty of resurrecting my childhood.
But aren't we all pimple faced,
buck-toothed at the mirror,
four eyes sliding down the nose,
playing cards on bicycle spokes
to make our own engines go?

What makes the Hottentot so hot?
Who put the ape in apricot?

My mother adjusts the radio knob,
it's Martha & The Vandellas' "Dancing in the Street"
and through the twilight of car lights
I tell her that these are the season's last fireflies,
the finale, the closing curtain call, the grand good bye.
All the clichés my life has been;
love as rose apple the eye,
armadillo I once rolled over
into a fire ant's mound.

I am Paladin in the back seat
calling card, clothes-pin gun,
black stetson and matchstick moustache.
The highway's coda before me,
the telephone poles that barricade me in,
the mad lights that buzz their algebraic colors
across the car's vinyl canopy.
I roll down the window
wind blow the great west's dust roar.
I got a plan.
I got a plan see,
to get us all out of here.

Sanatorium, 1977

I

Pleas Coulter thumps his hands
against the trunks of his legs.

                           The old bachelor farmer

looks up smiling
fingers crip
        pled
jig sawed
        jaun
              diced
and accu
        satory (N)ails brit tle a shag ged
                                  pa
                                      tina

thighs a ruddy channel
of bruised
craters

                          His sister's thorazined in the ward

above him

                                  haphazard ponytail

simple and docile   in blue
in her hospital   gown
she is angelic
her freckles

                          erupt into scars.

II

The state senator
the orderlies call "Mister"
has large ears   once
owned a bicycle shop I had heard

51

He is in need
                    of a bath.

I smear the pod
of his wrinkled body
with betadine
consider how it browns
the billows of steam,
paints the hot water
that will scald this public soaking.
Patch of gray hair *sur la tête*
curly pubic mass
octopus-like below
the waist.

                              I conduct him in
                              as if he were a liner
                              sternward toward
                              a sleeping dock.

Stoic and entrenched by the tub's clinical rim.

I wield harsh brushes
to shred the skin raw,
witness the plumage
of soap bubbles
the momentary pop
of rainbow colors.

It is my back that concerns me
my spine unused to strain of curve spine
of long extended bends, brown water
sloshing against my uniform white.

Pulling the drain
I prepare
to engage in
my heavy lifting.

I am slow to grab
the harsh
white towel,
to dry him
from the vulnerability
of industrial air.
His eyes witness
my discrepancies

                    knows my attentions have been amiss

that in between the billows of steam
my arm pulling and hand tugging
have all been on the clock.

"Boy." "Boy?" he says to me repeatedly

                              (eyes incredibly blue)

in a far-off tone that speaks
to neither my age nor race.

A narrative stitch in cosmic sound
that momentarily bridges the void
of our lost and lonely lives.

The Implausibility of Rabbits

The carrot cigar with the rabbit
wiggles dentures at the class door

Ms. Ross waves her yardstick
stretches polyester pulp in her pants.

Robert totes a bandaged thesaurus
of phantom entomologies, spit-sputters
bugs bunny 'sup doc tha' tha' that's
all she wrote 'Teach'
Bit the hare of the rabbit
that bit me.

He smells of sour feta and black olive.

We're regimented to sit in stiff back
rows of compass point carved blue
pen stained desks chalk dust mirage.

Wasn't it pigtailed Williams, Sharon S. first said
she adored him, but not their initials carved.

"You're in a world of pretend," Ross says.
Gray chapeaux tips the rabbit.

In the corner the stars
and bars are blooming.
All along Robert's been a diminutive
patriot singing God Bless
America Columbia the Gem of the Ocean.

Here comes 1940 Peter (Ellington)
Cotton tail of thee he sings
He desires taproot and beta carotene,
that Ross vaporize in suburban stew.

The bell announces a new period

All along beyond here lies nothing
All along great buckets of lotuses
swollen by rain.

IV
9 /ˈlīvz 9/ ˈlīnz

overheard

i remember water
white spray
& jutting
rocks   I look
ahead
measure sweat
from   the neck
in front
of me

accord

daddy
left me
this guitar
        a string's
busted
      but
it's a fine
one
        ain't it

Fin de Siècle

bus st
        op
five am
automobile
cruzin' by
(just
        waitin')
for the bus
to get here?

Security(%)Scrutiny

before i
walk into
any space,
i check first
to see
if there
are any
black people
there

neighbor boy

Charlie Frizzle
once told
me
i look
like a
chocolate
ice-cream cone
with jimmies
on top

incident

In high
school
The dark skinned
Greek
kid
made it
clear

when he called me
nigger.

live lyre

Mr. Woodworth
the toupee
wearing choral
director
warned me
my "power to
the people"
button was
too incendiary

interview

"and you are so
articulate"
was the ass-end
of a backhanded
compliment dispensed
by a business man
who prided himself
on his ability to discern
my curriculum vitae

M. N. (original recipe)

1. & in
2. some
3. places
4. i have
5. been
6. known
7. to be
8. magic
9. ...

V

\ ' fä-li-kəlz \

Reprise

This night draped in a red beard of clouds
speckled in the star grey stubble
I mistake for the twirling firmament of your eyes.

I am caught by them when suddenly you look up
as if to catch the turbulence of an impending storm
where words to convey my loss are irretrievable.

This night that swallows the howl of tree limbs
fringed in leaves, cupping a crescent of insects.

This night with its promises to be like no other
lies in wait licking its paws.

This black night that does not stand for ceremony
and sit on the brink of surrender.

I cannot count the spasms of my tongue
buttressing probe against my teeth
I cannot count the evasions of follicles
scalloped by a night wind.
I call out to it in whispers
as I would a lover.

Come out dear Luna.
Come fourth dear Nuit.
I beseech you as a supplicant
offering you the bitter fruit of my language.

Oh what am I getting at Night?
You who sleep oblivious to the world of lovers.
You angelic schemer.
Complicit in withholding from
me the crater peaks that disrupt
the surface of my emerging moon.

Seasonal

Every fallen petal diminishes spring — Tu Fu

Your accent suddenly sculpted
by pedestrians abreast of you.

Indeed you are sublime
whimsical even,

with your firecracker hair your
meteoric eyes your

post-colonial cheekbones your
spasm of sound erupting

from your throat

your gelded walk
straight out the gate.

I look up from papers
across pavements blown

a nation of headlines composed.

On the corner the partisans nod
ride the urban breeze
brimmed by your banter.

But the boutique's display window

reveals you for what you are
a Madison Avenue reflection receding

a living mannequin wreathed in
pelts of 21st century materialism.

I can think of no other way to say this.

To insult my mammal kin
to say you are dog, or ape, or pig
is to lower their standing
on the great cosmic wheel.

But I was born a singer and
to pepper my narrative with images
tosses this song to the marketplace.

Who am I to speak
spewing my accusations to come
raining down in a coinage of words.

We are complicit
in the joy we receive from
each other's suffering.

All of us at one time,
taking up the begging bowl.

Circa 1902, from the French

Annabelle, you are not of this world
with its skids and skirmishes
its abominations of automobile and asphalt.

From your perch the city
writhes and bleeds and dances
in the tongues of steam.

It is a conjecture of narratives
that no one is interested in.
Least of all you in your bloomers

of faded lace, your flowered bodice clasped
with safety pins and prayers.
In the grainy print the dandies slip by

their long legs and leather boots
plow through what looks like
the aftermath of rain.

In the film Annabelle,
a voiceover tells me what to think.
It is not you on the divan in the parlor

where sunlight filters through
nor you on the bench waiting with a crowd
for slow moving trolleys.

The camera draws in closer to reveal
the rouge on your cheek
which is gray and ghostly.

It is moving away from you.
The celluloid print is yellowing.
Outside it is 2019, your story long ended.

the eye doctor who doesn't see
Strawberry Festival, Roanoke, VA.

The street can be a kind of chart
where cars come straddling through.
White lines, store signs
they move to the cross & go.

But not for my optometrist
who stubbornly forges ahead
diaper bag on one arm
pink stroller on the other
and with a wife who
looks just as young as he.
I imagine them carded
to embarrassment, even to anger.

By now the clouds are beginning
to rumble in and it looks like
the glob of festival goers
have devoured their strawberry
shortcake and carbs.

Not my intrepid eye doctor
who negotiates his way through
a throng, a crowd, a mass, a congregation,
a cloud lumbers by
maybe my doctor imagines
a green valley with blue
stream running through
nymphs and naiads asleep in the pollen.

He does not hear our drumming,
fails to see Rudy playing out
rhythms for his murdered son.
Does not see the dangers of returning
to Mexico city that Pepe foresees.

He will not regard
a nation of drummers
beating at the gates.

the hotel worker

Hemmed in

                              by her uniform
she carefully extracts loose change
                    from her pockets.

Places it

              in Pepe's crocheted hat
                    on the sidewalk
                    (dollar bills spill out
                    like loose autumn
                    foliage)

She bends over, nestles floating currency
with the grace that defied conquistadors.

Surrounded she is, by the space of our drumming,
these itinerant rhythms whispering flashes of light

                    (a crowd snakes through the scene)

She sprinkles the coins.
She rains them down.
                    She flicks her wrist
                    makes the music her own.
She has given us the
              w r
            ea (l)
              th

                    of her
work.

and when she smiles
              She gives it back to us
and when she smiles

77

he give it back to us

VI
\ ˈmi-dᵊl \

IV

/ ʕb-im /

t/here it is

Somebody once told me/towed me/trolled me
"Where there's a Will
there's a way!"
(was what he said)
and i got to thinking
this Shakespeare thing has gone way too far
and what kind of weight
was he even talkin' bout?
That's like being lassoed with a lariat of lyrics.

(My god, that was during the Trump years
when people's (s)hackles were up.)

Let me be clear
Let me be Claire
Let me be Clorox
Let me be celestial
Let me be corpus
Let me be chorus
Let me be cavalier
cause that's the only currency
I got

See, there is some thing

(and he got it all mixed up)

See, there was some think
See there was some shenanigans
something sinister afoot

and yet, and yet , and yet, and yet, and yet, and yet, and yet, and yet, and yet
and yet, and
yet,

the rhythm shifts in

and the soul gets to blazing *boom*
and they say

"Who do the sayin'?"

81

Something in the rhythm
that morphs this phantom body
into a two-step dance between
the legs of Papa Legba holding
his cane up for me
I pour libations for him
He greets me at the crossroads

My dance contains
my own buck and wing
part goat part eagle

with arms waving aloft
they could be appendages
they could be hard handled knifes

There is no need to offer an explanation of the folktale
about Black people flying. There is scientific proof that
they did. Eye witness accounts reveal that people lifted
up from the ground. One man reported seeing a yellow
glow arising from the bottom of their feet. "I looked up
and saw one woman disappear into the clouds," he said.

There is

Snakehips Tucker's serpentine swirl
cross supper club dance floors in the 20s

That's got to remind you of

the middle the middle the middle
the muddle the middle the middle
the middle the middle the middle
the muddle the middle the middle
(*passage*) (past out) (passed own)

Passed on from one mouth to another
from palms that stun the skins
set them to singing true

seafaring, sea foraging

see: underwater: as in house or body
but not articulated complex completed
.⁻ ..⁻. .⁻. .. ⁻.⁻. .⁻
blink blink blink dash dash dash dot dot

At the Black and White Ball (Boston, 1980s)
Guillermo shows up wearing a tux and a life vest.
Judy straddles up to him.
"Who you s'ppose to be," she says.
"I'm a man lost at sea."
"How can I help you?" she whispers in his ear.
"You can't. I'm drowning! I'm drowning!" he replies.

                           and all that reels into

hauling goods, that reels into being goods,
that reels into hulls Caribbean bound
that reels into *hush little baby don't you*
cry *The Stars Fell over Alabama that night*

Ever heard of the Virginia Reel?

Was it *Last night, Night before*
Twenty-four robbers at my door
Not Aladdin's forty thieves
dank cave laden with fancy jewels
the genie at the entrance entranced
emeralded (really?)
                    (Is that the Jeanie you dream of?
                    She of *the light brown aire, I mean hair*)
                    Jeanie? How casual
                    and familiar you sound.

The prescription is the trance the prescription is the rhythm the prescription is
the trance the medicine is the rhythm the perception is the trance the medicine
is the rhythm the trance the trance the trance the trance the medicine the
protection

83

that the drum calls up
is the fount, is the font, is the front, is the funk
is the fury, is the fit, is the flirt, is the fete,
is the foretold
the tribal memory found
saying come children
don't you get weary
let's laugh, let's weep,
let's remember together.

Sitting on my Side Porch Reading Ramanujun
For Srikanth

Source fed:
>a cicada's electric sass
>>foretells this land brimmed in shards
is jaundiced by the murmur of diesel.

A tsunami of decorative savanna grass lunges
through a crevice in our deck
& sprouts tendrils.

Like fingers they writhe, devouring the day's
stitching.

The people next-door are being patient

>>with each other.

On a dark night, I hear him tell her
"We see the same moon."

Soon the acceleration of fall will   *& I will know her by her phases*
have us routed. Soon those cicadas   *she has set the table*
will surrender their seven years of waiting. *for feasting and*
                                            I have watched for signs
                                            in her branches

No longer will they disrupt the inquisitive moan
of a mourning dove gesturing her feathers
to the ground littered with scavenger ants.

They will not deceive my black cat
who slovenly springs   to the window's edge
with perked ears
& a taste for delight.

I hear the whirl of an airplane overhead.   *But I see the raptors*
Perhaps a passenger absentmindedly stirs a cup of tea *silk road booty*
oblivious to steam rising in a pressurized cabin. *replica of Thoreau's Walden*

And we will find ourselves lonely
among plasma screens and keyboards,
reconstituted minerals and earthen flame.

How I long to experience
just that kind of pressure.

I am simply that
a community of cells
blood molten & metallic
horn said to be
the inventor of jazz
flatted fifth this life/live

A Mist Consumes

Adamic, my desire to name things
to traverse a veil of atmospheric condensation
to postulate that something lies
in wait on the other side of this cumulus.

To label it gray
to call it dismal
to say it's gray and dismal
to refer to it as boredom's cadence.

I settle into the despondency of foliage
my desperate scheme to create
the sustenance of image or memory
where no rhododendron blood bloom will haunt
what propelled me into this orchestrated rising.

Everything is confiscated
by the unopened attaches of branches
by leaves arabesqued
or the silhouettes of joggers, water colored
in wash grey-blur.
Here, no statuesque sycamore nor oak opaquely
stamped to border land and sky.

My language is a neural passageway
a cerebral sextant hoisted from the coffers
of verb and noun, a transatlantic straddle
nasal not naval
a whiff, a smell I'm attuned to.

For the moment, it's the walk
the projective pulse of my body on pavement
the insistent tug of my imagined appointments
headed morning lit towards
the abyss of my upcoming years
as this planet saunters through constellations.

Distracted, I ignore the lacrosse field plowed by cleats
the compost of upturned clover and earthworm
the quartz and granite fumed pathway
that tongue the soles of my sneakers
the barn stack spewing flocks
of mourning dove and pollution colored pigeons.

Undeterred, I zip up my coat
walk through an amber cloak of leaves
not knowing if I have foretold
my own passing or am moving
towards something entirely new.

The Language of Faculty Meetings

⁓

Procedural   fault line(s)
              :di ver sion s)   tabled
to distant border(s
          boulders
ephermal *spac* iaL(s)
        facials

⁓

Motion(s exfoliate(d
        No, expose(d
               No, "x" spouse(s) (ed)
voca
   bularies s/play(ed)
           constellation(s   arseniced
No, arsenaled
                       Who's in control here?
constable/   con stable/
           :conceptacle:

*

Language stock piled
spew(ed) by degree*
           decree
a. to stay root**ed**
b. to stray rout**ed**
c. to spray rustic
               not this ram rod dying in the, in the,
in the, Oh
do not go gentle into that   Good Night!

Colonial *Continental*

Shuffle

{Don't you know everybody's doing it!}
Syntax singed   *sin tax?*   Credential[ed]
crop combine(d   cop/ped a feel *a flicker a filigree a filly*
for *Robert's Rules*
harvest (ed. It al

⸻

a mine of mixed grammar(s
a mind of nixed glamor(s

)
(t(he

:lectern:
)

Ivory no, ivy pillar   *pill or...*
mirror pilferer   voltive   voltaic   volley(ed)
where multiple variants exist *exit*
in space, in place
of a discipline specific

⸻

Diploma dis\in cline(d
To kinder(ed)
to kin
No, you're too kind
Too collegial too congenital   this
handshake, shook, shuck, shoot, souk   shit!
Scratch my synonym
Oil my suffix
Prime my prefix, my prefect, my parliamentary predilection
Solitary this
Soil this
call to odor.

90

Dr. Martin Luther King Jr. Day
January 15, 2000, Roanoke, Virginia

Instructions to a lady I know:

It is not ok to say
"Happy Lee-Jackson-King Day!"
to the solitary African American professor
crossing the quad in cotton and books.

Not good form to utter
through a saccharine smile   of teeth falsed

to mindlessly spew the import
of words haphazardly lodged
while the wet mortar of slave levied masonry
holds white columns of ivy stripped
buildings full of genealogies and diplomas (rinse and repeat).

No, not proper etiquette to whistle
            "I'm a Dixie Doodle Dandy!" (baton and casserole in
hand)
whilst Black folks scrape your plates
trim your lawns and gardens
arrange your stars and stripes
your pubic gnomes.

Not ok to tip your brim,
to wave your hand
in a "heartfelt" salute
to multicultural cheer

            while citizens get shackled off
            to penitentiaries to manufacture your continual
            comfort of feigned camaraderie and consent.

It is indeed bad juju to append the name
of the good doctor

on the end
of your noose
laden sentence

while you dig up your relics of gray
under the burning embers of postcards

where poplar and bodies swung.

Tell me then, where is the balm of peace,
the unspoken joy of a sunset with no complications?
The church sister whose contralto voice whirls
cosmos bound to raise the rafters filled
with the righteous who will heal this blessed earth.

In 1965 when the man died
I was a khaki-shorted seven-year-old
coming in after a day of riding
my bicycle between backyard
alleys and gravel driveways.
Once home, I remember Huntley and Brinkley's
sepia glow lined up against the silhouetted
face of my mother weeping
as news bulletins rolled in like thunder.
No need to say it was prophesy. We all knew it!

Yesterday while sailing down a Buchanan county lane
I feared the car would run out
of gas and I would be adrift
on the high seas of your
lynching roads where
the last thing I saw
was a barbed wire compound
shrouded in a looming X and a truck
loaded with celebratory beer and confederate cheer.

So lady, tell me if you can
what is the dream you
bequeath to me

with your sinister smile,
and your lopsided passing?

Picaresque

Blue Ridge Mountain
push up. The Tsalagi
called it *Shah-con-ah-jey*
meaning *Land of the Blue Mist*

green hills
gold trees
oak leaf temples

clouds that swirl
swallowtails floating
above dandelion line

what was that like?

VII

\ ˈker-ə-ˌpās ,ˈka-rə- \

Site Specific

I

The measurements for Cappuccino
should be fluid like jazz.

One starts with music
Attention to clef signature, tempo,
and bridge, the opening up of space
in the collective sigh of the downbeat

Hey Sylvia. You set the table.
Call it like you see it
as if you were corralling the kids
in for dinner or the elders for a night of pinochle

II

Sitting on the mantle
this ornamental mug champions
the history of my tribe.
My uncle brought it back
from Atlantic city, walking
on the boardwalk with a wife
that was not his own.
Now it's a carapace for the froth
of our arguments, my refusal to part
with my mannish ways.

A certain camisole
of whipped sugar poised as surf.
This drink evokes the satin plumes of paradise
Tell me, what was her name?

III

The view from Lonnie's tenement
revels in splattered class, busted
street lamps, rusted engine blocks
cracked graffiti on sidewalk streets
"whatever" has been played out
long ago & the doorbells sound
in minor keys & a pigeon struts
& dances in the carnage of lottery
tickets. "My God," Lonnie says
surveying his kingdom.

The limbs that settle
orchestrated in the silica of heat.

IV

Sylvia is from sea joints specializing in hot air pot or postage or portage
or porridge, a ridge of teeth to latch to, part of a chance shanty a song
to the special rayon of mandible ants in my uncles' basement. This here
rest is molar, this be upward mobility arrested sand, a gallant embassy of
pines, an hour when the scalpers tumble their silhouettes from the sky.
The temperature is brusque, is aquiline is the hat check maid in the leper
leap who scours toes an angle worthy of chivalry and taking our orders.
Counter of malfunctions that key the bones play in the dog muzzle up
to the lap, wins the top blue prize. Sylvia closes her vespers and whispers
of night while the poor frost puts a remedy of ills in the aurora of our
throats. Don't sever fate. Tap the table that judges the dinner. Sylvia, take
up your own horn!

VIII

\ 'ta-pə-strē \

On Hearing Cecil Taylor

Like a Like a Like a Like a Like a Like a piston
plunging into bayou depths of sunken treasures hulled of black bodies
Like a humming bird strategically perched strategically perched
on a cocaine's dropper Like a like a like a second shift fry cook
at a two o'clock grill On a sat On a sat On a Sat-ur-day burn
Like a hand sprinkled with the olfactory stench
of smoke stack sailors on shore ship leave
Like a Bolden tremolo to a flapper's piss poor smile in Funky Butt Hall
Like a gore. Like a Goree Like a Goree chain Like a Goree chain step.
Like a Goree Island chain step.
Like a city skull-scraper holding up blue sky in a razor's twinkle

Still the road Still the road Still the road to evolutions evolving to the
pageantry of ancestral breath and bone at the crossroads
of Julliard and Johnson
where the devil gives up his hold of the music
Still the road Still the road Still the road where the scale is the song in a
bison's bladder Where the scale is the song in a bison's bladder
Where the alphabet is the shrapnel of consonants
a firefight piano's blur in the cockleburs of your chest
a wind piped whole note on the cobblestone of cadenzas

Like a Like a Like a Like a A, Like a Ahhh, Like a Ahhh. Like a huh, Like
a huh, Like a ma like a ma, like a mah like mah mah like a Mau Mau like a
Mau Mau
Like a starlit moon orbiting the balcony
Like a girl getting up   leaving her seat   slamming the theater door

Baby don't you know you can't step out of the cosmos.

Visions of Jimmy

"Are you a he or a she?" divisively spoken
in a bar obscured by low crawling light.
Little Jimmy at the microphone stand,
holding it as if it was
Papa Legba's crossroad staff
or a tropical palm frond up
against the backdrop of the Nile
or Moses with his staff of snakes.

"But ahh the couture velour of his voice," an aficionado decrees
"Just sends me man, just sends me..," someone whispers close eyed

Some called him The Source
The Singer's Singer. Not the oddity
who would later Twin Peak them
in their late night dreams.

"Little Jimmy got small balls
and one night, stripped
in an Atlanta holding tank
four white cops laughing,
"another unfortunate nigger."
The anecdote arrives with laughter
It arrives with tears.

Jimmy Scott gracile and stealth behind
the piano's tapestry, a bass man laying out
the tune's bottom, a drummer polishing
high hat's shimmer, a horn player
emptying a valve of spit.

Scott unraveling the ornament,
delivery held aloft, sullen but
always on point like
the breath's intake on a joint
followed by the reluctant
trickle of gray smoke

or the lone water bead skating
down a glass of booze.

Little Jimmy at the microphone
in his black tux, shiny.
Looking like a young kid
to an audience of drinkers.
"Hey man, saw you in Cleveland. Made me cry."
"Hey man, balled my baby after hearing
you with Hamp." More consolatory
in their minds.

*

Little Jimmy signing recording contracts
singing at funerals
working as an elevator operator
pushing buttons in 60s three star hotels,
"You going down Mam?"
"Don't I know you?" she says.

Little Jimmy in a night club
behind the wings,
the room throbbing.
Fathead just finished the opening,
pulls the reed out, wipes his brow.
Big Mabelle long gone
When she died so heavy
they had to cut out her bedroom door
to drag her out.

Where do they come from?
All anxiously at their tables,
chattering and holding their cigarettes,
clinking and nursing their two drink minimums.
Little Jimmy now ready to go on.

"Excuse me, son," says some woman

"Can you tell me where the
Ladies Room is?"
Little Jimmy smiling
tells her, "It's hard to get there
from here. I'll show you."

He's gone.
Now he's back
Stepping up and out to the mic
and into the place where we see
and don't see him.

That Kind of Summer

For my mother, Lois Fields Anderson

I

On the Jersey's shore
where fools
       (i mean waves
           like a rage of starlings
           or seagulls, your temperament depending)
rush in

In that kind of sand footstep imprints
sun tan oil and discarded magazines
faded markers to a presence, a presence, a presence, *(calling back now)*
this imagined witness to see you
held in the golden cloak of time

To know those moments

           when water's froth perkled blue
            and kelp curls curved
            and petals of white Bivalvia shells
             littered the seascape

           Your tiptoed waltz in the luminescence
a showering of bubbles
and salt taffy air
                If you put a shell
                to your ear
                you'll hear
                that ancient music

Evening approaches and sun yields to twilight
Candlelit boats bounce
and buoy in the distance

to siesta lap of water's rhythm
nestling in the ear of this ocean song.

II

It is summer.
You are working at a resort
you are washing dishes
that are not your own

Suds and hot mist obscuring
your view of the dining hall
where Billy Eckstine's velvet baritone—
has cut through the tourist chatter

> *Our little dream castle with every dream gone*
> *Is lonely and silent, the shades are all drawn*

(I wonder what those people were wearing?
Were they smoking, eating salt peanuts,
nursing cocktails, adjusting mascara,
eyeing each other's date?)

One can't help but think
of that handsome man
with debonair styled suits
draping over him
like luminous clouds

Could you see the sea from your restaurant post?
Could you hear Eckstine's voice cut through the steam,
the applause, the weather?

Space is the Place

in honor of Sun Ra

Calling planet earth
Calling planet earth

It's time we return to our cosmic altars
We've made the best of this earth
Given it our music and acumen

P/Raised up ancestral wisdom
across this journeyed terrain

Danced in jooks
      in churches
        in temples
and discos
                    Genuflected our way after
                    that mid-court shot
                    where we sent the ball
                    skyward like a Mende prayer

Where we wielded pigments and clay
to finger, to figure, to fugue a future
of continual, contemplative set
of ancestral witness

                    Crisscrossed our way over
Atlantic foam and hydro-curl

                    Carried the b(st)ones of our families
to the Americas
where we were auctioned
into the arms of Europe's greed

            Seen by people settled in longhouses
                whose visions predicted

                              such a such a such a such a horrific
devouring

                                        But before that
                                        we traveled
                                        the space ways
                                        where all celestial
                                        beings dervished
                                        their divine dances
                                        and were brilliant

Our legacy is resistance
Our legacy is survival

and I mean to tell you that
                    we are both here
                                   and out there
                                            the same time.

110

Gambit

For Ira Clayton Eshleman Jr.

when I start to think
about it
it vanishes

when I start
thinking
about it
it goes like this
           he began to sing
a way *a long way home*
sometimes I feel

(this passion, I mean

to create a life
out of fissures

           he began to sing again
all of me why not take all of me

This morning I went to the fridge
to retrieve my breakfast in cartons
and plastic bowls prepared bananas
and yogurt
           he began to sing
I'm Popeye the sailor man. Toot! Toot!

& don't you know god is Bud Powell?

           he began to sing again
my bonnie lies over the ocean
my bonnie lies over the sea
oh bring back my bonnie
to me to me

He began to sing.

The meat was on the counter.
He began to sing.

Mary of Witness

for Great Grandma Mary Tusker

Black hair loose strands
Wood spoon to stir the stew
Thumbnail ragged
from scrubbing
Oh Mary
Oh Mary don't ya weep.

Oh Mary
Ledge on window
Day Lilly in the pot
Pantry floor painted white
Oh Mary don't ya weep.

Mary of apron and scarf
Mary of womb and scab
Mary known simply to me
as a name on great granddaddy's death papers
Oh Mary
Don't you weep

Oh Mary don't you weep no last sunset
in the dark spectacle of your eyes
Oh Mary don't you buckle no last shoe
in the empty sockets of your calloused feet.
Oh Mary. Don't you take no dimes
No dollar eagles to weigh your lids.

Oh Mary mother of Kudzu
of periwinkle and stone
of quartz cloudy as puss
Oh Mary the unmarked past
eats at the crevices in my hands
Oh Mary don't you weep.

Oh Mary don't you weep

Ravens crouch on oak limbs
Their sleek black beaks
are miraculously silenced
by the mere mention of your name.

IX

\ 'wāt \

involuntary shutter

The muscle
in my thigh
has set to wiggling
again like an angry
old man jawing
his way across
the boulevard.

It's winter,
my skin easily ashen
a crevice of gray
canyons and dry rivers
in need of rain.

My thigh has commenced
to thumping and dancing
under the vulgarity of its own weight.

Ashamedly slinking down
in the direction of my
ankles like a badly behaved child.

What I really want to relay
could not be spoken
due to my teeth slamming
against my tongue.

Prayer

candle light i am breath
breath & brain
& bone & muscle

i am a darter snail mid-river
a whisper freshly evaporating
from the w/holy month of your mouth.

In the stillness t/here
is nothing to say.
The birds of paradise roost

in our heads.
This is what they call
mind at full nest.

Notes

"Oble Tombou"
Oble Tombou *refers to an accelerated drum rhythm/pattern that is used to evoke the arrival of the* loa *(loosely translated as "spirits").*

"Fast Talking Hombre"
This poem was influenced by the work of Maria Sabina, a Mazateca sabia *from the Mexican state of Oaxaca and Anne Waldman's "Fast Talking Woman."*

"Visions of Jimmy'"
Jimmy Scott was an American jazz vocalist famous for his unusually high contralto voice, which is due to Kallmann syndrome, a very rare genetic condition. The condition stunted his growth at four feet eleven inches until, at age 37, he grew another 8 inches to the height of five feet seven inches. The condition prevented him from reaching puberty, leaving him with a high, undeveloped voice, hence his nickname "Little" Jimmy Scott.
See David Ritz's biography: *Faith in Time: The Life of Jimmy Scott*

Dedication

Grateful acknowledgement is extended to the following people: Pauline, Yasmine, & Céline for co-creating the kind of home that makes this work possible; my parents, T.J. and Lois Anderson, who continue to remain the inspirational guides on my journey; my sisters, Anita and Janet, who bring joy and laughter to me; my dear brother, Joseph Torra, who had his ear to my work for such a long time; the brilliant William Repass whose insights into this manuscript have given it energy and life; Srikanth Mallavarapu, a scholar of eclectic tastes and fellow jazz traveler; John McDonald, my brother whose conversation and music continue to inspire; the incomparable Bill Banfield, who brings energy to everything he does; the marvelous community of makers I encountered at MacDowell and the Virginia Center for the Creative Arts and under the arches of the Memorial Street Bridge; the dynamic community of Hollins University my academic home; and to Rusty Morrison and my Omnidawn family who treat my work with wonder, respect, and care.

I am grateful for my poetry lineage, and I have been the recipient of valuable lessons from those who have given me the tools to shape this work: Lloyd Schwartz, Richard Tillinghast, Milton Kessler, Isidore Okpewho, and Clayton Eshleman. Appreciation is extended to the many teachers I encountered in books and readings.

Gassho to the teachings of the non-human. May I learn to listen and use them wisely.

Publication Acknowledgement

Versions of some of these poems have appeared in other venues. Grateful appreciation and acknowledgement is extended to the following publications: *Big Other, Rabbit: a Journal of Non-fiction Poetry, Let the Bucket Down, Resisting Arrest: Poems to Stretch the Sky,* and *The Future of Black: Afrofuturism, Black Comics, and Superhero Poetry.*

photo by Céline Anderson

Born in Guthrie, Oklahoma, poet and musician T.J. Anderson III is the author of *Devonte Travels the Sorry Route* (Omnidawn Press, 2019), *Cairo Workbook* (Willow Books, 2014), *River to Cross* (The Backwaters Press, 2009), *Notes to Make the Sound Come Right: Four Innovators of Jazz Poetry* (University of Arkansas Press, 2004), *Blood Octave* (Flat Five Recordings, 2006), and the chapbook *At Last Round Up* (lift books, 1996). He has had fellowships with The Virginia Center for the Creative Arts (VCCA) and The MacDowell Colony. He teaches at Hollins University in Roanoke, Virginia.

photo by Celine Anderson

t/here it is
by T.J. Anderson III

Cover art by Joseph Epps

Cover typeface: Futura
Interior typefaces: Garamond and Futura.

Cover design by Laura Joakimson and
Interior design by Ken Keegan

Printed in the United States

Publication of this book was made possible in part by gifts from
Katherine & John Gravendyk in honor of Hillary Gravendyk,
Francesca Bell, Mary Mackey, and The New Place Fund

Omnidawn Publishing
Oakland, California
Staff and Volunteers, Spring 2022

Rusty Morrison & Ken Keegan, senior editors & co-publishers
Laura Joakimson, production editor and poetry & fiction editor
Rob Hendricks, editor for *Omniverse,* poetry & fiction, & post-pub marketing
Sharon Zetter, poetry editor & book designer
Jeff Kingman, copy editor
Liza Flum, poetry editor
Anthony Cody, poetry editor
Jason Bayani, poetry editor
Gail Aronson, fiction editor
Jennifer Metsker, marketing assistant
Jordyn MacKenzie, marketing assistant
Sophia Carr, marketing assistant